A LAWYER'S GUIDE TO A TAX-FREE RETIREMENT

BY JORN ROSSI

Published by

Green Door Investment Properties LLC

30 N. Gould Street, Suite R

Sheriden, Wyoming

Copyright @ 2018 Jorn Rossi / Green Door Investment Properties LLC

ALL RIGHTS RESERVED

PRINTED IN THE USA

ISBN 13: 978-1987569957

ISBN 10: 1987569954

All rights reserved. No part of this publication may be reproduced, stored in a retrieval system, or transmitted in any form or by any means, electronic, mechanical, photocopied, recorded, or otherwise, without the prior written permission of the publisher.

This publication is designed to provide general information regarding the subject matter covered. Because each individual's legal, tax, and financial situation is different, specific advice should be tailored to the particular circumstances. For this reason, the reader is advised to consult with his or her own attorney, accountant, or other financial advisor regarding that individual's specific situation. The author has taken reasonable precautions in the preparation of this book and believes that the information presented in the book is accurate as of the date it was written. However, neither the author nor the publisher assume any responsibility for any errors or omissions. The author and publisher specifically disclaim any liability resulting from the use or application of the information contained in this book, and the information is not intended to serve as legal, tax, or other financial advice related to individual situations

DEDICATION

To Connie, Lina, Von, Randoll and Mr. B. Thanks for everything. I love you. And thanks to Rocky and Miranda who inspire all of us to be all that we can be.

Table of Contents

I. THE SECRET 1
II. THE WEALTHY KNOW 3
III. THE FIRST STEP 5
IV. ONE OF A KIND 8
V. NEVER MISSED A PAYMENT 10
VI. TODAY'S MOTIVATION TO DO THE SMART THING 12
VII. KEY REQUIREMENTS OF THE PLAN 21
VIII. STARTING THE PLAN 43
IX. CONCLUSION 45

Illustration #1 Compounding Interest Rule of 72..13

Illustration #2 Money Taxed vs. No Tax..14

Illustration #3 Tax Now, Tax later, Tax Free..16

Illustration #4 Gain Needed To Recover From a Loss.................................22

Illustration #5 With a "floor" You Never Lose Money...................................25

Illustration #6 $624,400.00 in and get back $4,096,888.00........................35

Illustration #7 $336,169,22.00 in and get back $4,478,702.00......................39

LAWYERS GUIDE TO A TAX-FREE RETIREMENT

I. THE SECRET

I have been an estate planning attorney for over 38 years. I know the secret – the secret of how to create a retirement savings plan that will provide the retirement of your dreams. Like a pirate's treasure map, this book will tell you how you get there: To a place where you do not have to work, where you have the money to pay your bills, where you have the money to travel, money to do what you want to do, to be with friends and family, a place to enjoy life in those "golden years", a place where there are no taxes.

This trip starts with knowing how to get there and then a plan of at what age you want to get there and with how much money. I tell my clients, if you cannot tell me at what age you want to retire at and with how much money, then you don't have a plan even if you think you know how to get there.

Few know how to get there. That is why almost half the future baby-boomer retirees are predicted they will not be able to afford to retire and in many cases, will be unable to work or find work, and will be unable to pay basic everyday bills. In this book I will tell you how to avoid this.

This book will change your life for the better. No doubt in my mind, and after you have read it, there will be no doubt in your mind.

You will only regret you did not know this before.

II. THE WEALTHY KNOW

Banks, giant U.S. corporations, many people who are rich, or who have become rich, know the way, know the secret, which is why they have the money they have and can do what they do. Let me ask you this: If wealthy people, who can do whatever they want to do with their money, are being advised by expensive attorneys and financial advisers to do what I recommend in this book, don't you think it must be a good way? Why else would they do it?

If you don't know how to get there you will have to have been very lucky in your life to get there. But, today, now, in this book, I will tell you. I will provide you with the map to a proven plan of growing wealth safely and predictably every year, without income taxation, and without loss, even if the stock market or real estate markets crash. A real wake up call to most, and if you do what I suggest and start the journey by creating your plan and start heading where you want to go financially in life, you will be heading there along the way without the financial stress and uncertainty most people live their entire life's with. A life time of fearing of how am I going to save enough money to retire? How am I not going to run out of money?

The greatest fear most people live with in retirement is: **Am I going to run out of money?**

Don't let this happen to you.

III. THE FIRST STEP

The first step is to open your mind to what I will tell you. Forget what you think you know, what others have told you, how it may have "use to have been". While what I will write in the following pages will be new to you, the strategy behind it actually is very old and proven. There are no risks. You will only make money, not lose it. There will guarantees you will not lose your savings. You will be able to stockpile your savings and be able to use it when you want and for any purpose. You will become your own banker, while your savings keeps earning and growing. Forget about applying for loans; forget about your FICO score. You alone will control your finances, and you alone, without Uncle Sam, will decide when you will spend your money and on what you will spend it on. You are the first beneficiary of this plan; it's all about you, and it will provide for you while you are alive, and after you have gone, for your family and future generations.

The secret to this is known as cash value life insurance.

Forget about what you thought about "life insurance" and the "death benefit" prospective peddled by most insurance agents. Today's cash value life insurance more than ever is about you and LIVING BENEFITS FOR YOU. It is not an investment, as will be explained, but a contract with a giant life insurance company to pay you, or loan you, a given amount of money at any given time, with the guarantee you will not lose money.

What I am going to tell you is the map to get to a tax free retirement and getting there with your savings always making money and on a tax-free basis making more with your savings then probably everybody else you know. No plan is safer, no plan is better, and after you have read this book you will agree – This is it.

Face it. If you follow what everybody else does, you will end up like everybody else. The fundamental problem is people invest in uncertainties, like the stock market, either directly or indirectly via though 401k, IRA, or other like government retirement plans. Who knows what will happen with the stock market? Truth be told, nobody knows. Investing in real estate, in a business, and in anything else, other than less-then-inflation-rate – low interest bank savings or CD's, is similar. There is a risk.

With the money you are saving for your retirement you do not want to take risks. You do not want to pay taxes on it either if you can avoid it. What you want to hear are guarantees and not some vague reassurance that it will turn out OK.

Today's cash value life insurance is about the living benefits to you now and when you retire and is based on a contract. It is not a security. It is not invested in the stock market. It is not some government plan which restricts your use of your money and requires you to pay income tax on it.

IV. ONE OF A KIND

What makes life insurance the one-of-a-kind investment it is, is because of IRS Code 7702. This tax code allows after-taxed dollars paid into a cash value life insurance policy to grow and to be spent without ever paying any income taxes on it – tax free.

No other investment vehicle can offer this. Money paid out of a 401k, IRA, or the like, has to pay income tax on it when used. At best these government retirement plans only defer your obligation to pay income tax. Sooner or later you are going to have to pay income tax on it. Probably at a higher income tax rate then now and at a time when you likely have fewer tax deductions which only makes it worst. Annuities are the same way. Tax deferment only. With annuities you have to pay income tax on every dollar you are paid. You will be paying income taxes when you retire. With cash value life insurance you never pay income tax or any tax of any kind when you use your savings because it is considered a loan and not income. Figure right there, your savings in a 401k, IRA, or in an annuity will be reduced 30% or more when you start using it to pay Uncle Sam his share. You thought the money in your annuity, 401k, IRA, or like government sponsored retirement plan was all your money. No way. You have a silent partner named Uncle Sam.

If instead, you had the same money in a cash value life insurance policy you will end up with 30% or more of your savings for you to spend during your lifetime because you do not have to pay income tax on it. This is just the start!

Besides not having to pay any future income tax, you are guaranteed not to lose money. Yes, guaranteed not to lose money. **No taxes and guaranteed you will not lose money. Two important phrases you want to hear when you talk about your retirement savings.** No taxes and no losing money. According to Warren Buffett, the billionaire investor, rule number #1 is never lose money.

V. NEVER MISSED A PAYMENT

The giant insurance companies like Transamerica, Nationwide, Prudential, Met Life, have never missed a payment. During the 1929 depression, the only investors who did not lose any money, actually kept making money were investors who had invested all or part if their savings in cash value life insurance.

When Walt Disney could not get bank loans to build Disneyland he borrowed against the cash value of his life insurance. Ray Kroc the owner of McDonald's to keep it going did not get paid for the first eight years. He lived off the cash value of his life insurance. J.C. Penny kept his stores open after the 1929 depression by drawing on his cash value in his life insurance. The Foster Farm family used their life insurance cash value to start the Foster Farm business. Bank of America, Wells Fargo Bank and most other large banks have invested billions and billions in cash value life insurance. Many if not most of the largest corporations you can think of, like Lockheed Martin, AT&T, Starbucks, General Electric, Anheuser-Busch, Verizon have put billions of dollars of their money into cash value life insurance. They all may tell you to save your money with them or use your money to buy their products but that's not what they are doing with their money, they are putting their money into cash value life insurance. Cash value life insurance is rated top tier #1 as a safe place to put your money.

In other words, what I am trying to tell you is smart people in the past and in the present put as much money as they can into cash value life insurance. After you have read this book, you will be smart too, you will put as much as you can onto cash value life insurance and money-wise your life is going to be much better.

VI. TODAY'S MOTIVATION TO DO THE SMART THING

Today, a person could live into their 90's so this creates a retirement savings problem. How are you going to fund a retirement that is likely to last 30 years? The biggest concern a retiree has and most live with is: Am I going to run out of money? Forget about it. Don't be one of those persons.

The fact that thanks to modern medicine and the evolving human body you are going to live longer then past generations creates a longer period for you to save for. So you have a bigger challenge then your parents to save for your retirement, This challenge is exacerbated by rising health care costs, expected social security decreases, and fewer employers offering retirement programs.

You will see the sooner you start on the smart tax free retirement plan I am telling you about, the less it will cost and the greater will be the amount you saved.

<u>Let's First Talk About How Money Works</u>.

The rate of interest you earn on your savings makes a big difference. As you can see from the classic financial "Rule of 72" chart, the rate of return makes a real big difference on how much you end up with. <u>See Illustration #1</u>.

Illustrations# 1 The Compounding Interest Rule of 72

Age 4%	Age 6%	Age 8%	Age 12%
Money doubles every 18 years	Money doubles every 12 years	Money doubles every 9 years	Money doubles every 6 years
29 $10,000	29 $10,000	29 $10,000	29 $10,000
47 $20,000	41 $20,000	38 $20,000	35 $20,000
65 $40,000	53 $40,000	47 $40,000	41 $40,000
	65 $80,000	56 $80,000	47 $80,000
		65 $180,000	53 $180,000
			59 $320,000
			65 $640,000

The amount of tax you have to pay on your savings makes a big difference too. As you can see from Illustration #2, the Money Taxed vs. No Tax Chart.

Illustration#2 Money Taxed vs. No Tax

ON 5% A YEAR GROWTH

YEAR	10K YEAR contribution	TAXED	NO TAX	difference WITH NO TAX
0	$10,000	0	0	0
5	$50,000	$56,300	$61,000	+4,700
10	$100,000	$131,800	$159,300	+27,500
15	$150,000	$232,700	$317,700	+$85,000
20	$200,000	$367,800	$572,700	+204,900
25	$250,000	$548,600	$983,400	+$434,800
30	$300,000	$790,500	$1,644,900	+$854,400

NO TAX ON GROWTH MAKES A HUGE DIFFERENCE

NO PLAN IS BETTER THEN A NO TAX PLAN

YOU DO NOT HAVE TO PAY INCOME TAX ON YOUR RETIREMENT SAVINGS

BE SMART - LIKE THE WEALTHY, LIKE WALT DISNEY WHICH WOULD YOU RATHER HAVE WHEN YOU RETIRE - $790,500.00 OR $1,644,900.00?

Historically, the tax rate mirrors governmental spending. The more the government spends the greater the tax rate. During World War II the spending was the greatest and the taxes were the highest. Today, the gap between what the United States government spends and what the government takes in from tax revenues has never been greater. How is that gap going to be reconciled? Most experts say by raising the current low tax rates higher to generate more income to lessen the gap between what the government spends and what it takes in.

Unless the U.S. economy grows like never before or cuts its operating costs like never before, raising taxes is the only way the U.S. is going to be able to pay its debts and pay its operating costs. That is why most financial planners today say you will be paying more income tax when you are retired then you are paying now. But you don't have to be an expert, ask anybody and they will tell you taxes are going up.

This government spending/income gap creates probably the most important planning decision you have to make:

Tax now, tax later, or no tax.

Illustrations #3 Tax Now, Tax Later, Tax Free

TAX NOW	TAX LATER	TAX FREE
Checking bank accounts	401(k) 403(b)	Roth-IRA
Savings bank accounts	IRA/SEP-IRA	529
CD'S	Pensions	7702
Stocks "Wall Street"	Social Security	
Mutual Funds	Annuity	
Rental Property Income	Investment Property 1031	

Take a look at Illustration #3. The "tax now" group is what most people do. The big problem with this is that yearly taxation keeps cutting down the amount of your savings so you have less savings growing. Another problem is whatever they invest in has the risk that they could lose it, like investing in the stock market. Their only other alternative is keeping their savings in low interest bank savings accounts or

CD's which earn less than the inflation rate which in reality is like losing money.

The "tax later" group, which all 401k, IRA, and other government retirement plans are in, is the worst group to be in, not only tax-wise but for many other reasons I will discuss later. While your income tax payment on your earnings is deferred so your savings is not reduced every year, so there is more principal earnings growing, the problem is that when you are allowed or required to withdraw the savings, you have to pay income tax not only on the original deferred earnings income tax, but will also have to pay income tax on the whole amount it has grown as you use it. You thought your retirement savings plan was all yours. No way. All this time you have had a silent partner named Uncle Sam who is going to share all your savings plus its earnings for all these years by taxing you when you take your money out at some unknown income tax rate, which as previously discussed will likely be at a much higher tax rate then what the income tax rate is at now. Making it worst, with your house hopefully paid off, and the kids then on their own, you will have less tax deductions to reduce this retirement income tax hit. It is problematic even for those who have saved a lot in these plans because the return on these savings will throw you into a higher tax bracket then you are now in.

I think it is safe to say, your savings in these plans are going to end up about a third (1/3) less then you thought they would be. I am sorry to have to be the one to tell you this.

As an aside, while we are on the 401k, IRA, type plans, I do recommend that you be in these plans to the point where you get matching funds from your employer, if they offer matching funds, as this is "free money", but once you reach the matching amount, don't put any more money in.

As another aside, if you are at the age 59 ½ to 70 ½, or soon will be, you might want to think about getting rid of your partner, Uncle Sam, by paying him off and joining the no tax group unrelated to Wall Street suggested in this book.

The last group, the "No tax" group is of course the best group and the group you want to be in. No plan is better than a no tax plan and the only way you can legally get into the "no tax" group is by putting your money in cash value life insurance thanks to IRS Code 7702.

Roth IRA's are in this "No tax" group, and while it is a big positive that they are not subject to tax later, Roth IRA plans have a lot of problems and are not recommended. You are restricted as to when you can access your money with the 59 1/2 age holding requirements and age 70 1/2 spending requirements, there are additional requirements as to how long you have had your Roth plan, and you are limited by how much you can contribute. Uncle Sam does this to prevent you from being able to do what you can only do under IRS Code 7702 with a cash value life insurance policy. In 2018, as of the writing of this book, other problems are you are limited to annual contributions of just $5,500.00 or $6,500.00 a year and if you make $135,000.00 a year as a single person, or $199,000.00 a year as husband and wife, you cannot even have a Roth IRA plan, and as with the other government retirement plans, Roth IRA's have no guarantees and most likely all the money you put into it will be put to risk on Wall Street.

Ok, now you know where you want to go. You want to go to the "no tax" group. Let's now talk about the plan.

VII. KEY REQUIREMENTS OF THE PLAN

The plan must offer the following: [1] safety, [2] growth, [3] tax benefit, [4] you control it, and [5] longevity.

Today's cash value life insurance policies are the only plans that can offer all this.

A. <u>Safety</u>

Good cash value life insurance policies I recommend, promise you will not lose money. The life insurance company promises you what is called a "floor". This is a guaranteed minimum amount your savings is going to earn no matter what. The floor on the policies I recommend promise a 0.75% interest rate per year on your money. 0.75% which is more than most banks are offering on savings accounts.

With a "floor" you will never lose money, which as I quoted Warren Buffet is Rule #1 in making money - Never lose money.

Making it even worst, when you take a loss, it may take many years to make your money back. Take a look at Illustration #4. If you lost 50% of your money it would require the stock market to gain 100% just to start making money again. How long, if ever, is it going to take the stock market to gain 100%? Nobody knows and we don't care because our plan is not going there. But for most people with their 401k's and IRA's, and even regular investors in the stock market, if the stock market drops 20% or more when you are retired it would be devastating – you just lost 20% or more of your retirement savings just when you need it. Not losing money can be just as important as making money.

Illustrations#4 Gain Needed To Recover From A Loss

GAIN NEEDED TO RECOVER FROM A LOSS		
-10% loss	requires a	**+11%** GAIN
-20% loss	requires a	**+25%** GAIN
-30% loss	requires a	**+43%** GAIN
-40% loss	requires a	**+67%** GAIN

> -50% loss   requires a   +100% GAIN
>
> Losing money is as important as making money. If you lose money the question is: How long is it going to take you to make it back, if ever? What are you going to do if this happens when you are retired and counting on it? Most retirement saving plans invest in the unpredictable, up and down stock market. Forget about it. You don't want to put your retirement savings at risk.
>
> **YOU WANT YOUR RETIREMENT MONEY IN A PLAN THAT GUARANTEES YOU WILL NOT LOSE MONEY. DOESN'T THIS MAKE SENSE?**

And not to be forgotten, in our plan not only do we not lose money and end up making a lot more money than the 401k, IRA stock market investor because of the "floor", the money we make is tax free so add another 30% to that amount!

b. <u>Growth</u>

In the cash value life insurance policies I recommend the insurance company promises to share the profits they made with your money up to a certain point. That point is called a "cap". Even though your money is not invested in the stock market, and even though the insurance company does not invest in the stock market, they gauge how much your yearly return will be based on a stock market index average up to the "cap" amount. For instance, the "cap" amount on the policies I recommend is 15% and is based on what is commonly called a "global index" which is the average of indexes of three different stock market indexes – the S&P 500, the Euro Stoxx 50 (the European stock market) and the Hang Seng (the Hong Kong – Asian stock market).

This means with the floor, you are going to make at least 0.75% up to 15% interest per year on your savings every year.

Illustration #5 shows the average 20 year return of the global index cash value life insurance policies I recommend with a 0.75% floor and 15% cap from 1995-2015 to average 9.03% per year. Without being in a 7702 cash value life insurance policy with the floor, the investment of the same amount of money in the S&P 500 index over the same period of time would have earned only 6.14% - almost a third less.

9.03% per year and no income tax on that. If you are in now or later a 30% income tax bracket you would have to make over 12% a year on your money to equal this. Did you do this? I doubt it. By the illustration averages we have looked at you likely made less than half this amount after paying income taxes.

Illustrations#5 With a "floor" you never Lose Money

Calendar Year	S&P 500 Index Change	Global Index Change using a **0.75% floor and 15% cap**
1996	19.33%	15.00%
1997	31.01	15.00
1998	26.67	15.00
1999	19.53	15.00
2000	-12.66	.075
2001	-10.53	0.75
2002	-23.37	0.75
2003	26.38	15.00
2004	8.99	8.59
2005	4.69	13.25

2006	11.65	15.00
2007	3.65	9.91
2008	**-38.49**	**0.75**
2009	23.45	15.00
2010	12.78	6.10
2011	1.54	0.75
2012	11.68	14.92
2013	29.60	15.00
2014	11.39	6.80
2015	-0.73	0.75
20 year average:	**6.14%**	**9.03%** **With a "floor" you never lose money. Makes a big difference.**

Also when you are comparing returns, if you add in the cost of term life insurance for the amount of death benefit that is included in the cash value life insurance policy, the cash value life insurance policy return is even greater. A lot greater and a lot better.

And last but not least, you live your life without the mental worries of how the stock market is doing, how much you are going to end up with, and what will be the amount of income taxes you will have to someday pay on it when you retire. In our plan, there are no future income taxes, your retirement savings are guaranteed. Your mind is on your golf score, where you are going on that next cruise, and when you will be seeing the grandchildren.

B. <u>Tax Benefit</u>

In our plan the reason you never pay income tax on your earnings is because under IRS Code 7702, when you take money out of your cash value life insurance policy it I not considered income. It is considered a "loan". A loan which you never have to pay back if you don't want to. What you do not take out and spend during your lifetime as a "loan", becomes a death benefit payment to whomever you choose and that too is income tax free. The net result is no income tax is ever paid. No other plan can offer this. Your plan has taken you from always taxed to never taxed. You can't beat that. No plan is better than a no tax plan.

Not to mention, if you use your insurance company loan for a business purpose, like buying a rental real estate property when the market tanks, the [low] loan interest can be written off as an expense increasing the rate of return on your investment!

C. <u>Control</u>

A big problem with 401k, IRA, Roth, and other government retirement savings plans are you have no control over your money, at least not without severe penalties. Under these plans you cannot take any money out until you are 59 ½ years old without paying income tax on it plus a 10% penalty. Likewise, at age 70 ½, you have to start withdrawing money or pay a penalty. With these plans if you need the money to buy a house, a car, college tuition, because you lost your job, to take advantage of a good investment because of a stock market or real estate market decline – forget about it. You can't get your money.

In our plan, you have complete control. You are your own banker. Whenever you want your money you can just call up the insurance company and tell them how much. Ten days or less you have the money. No questions asked. Not only that, you don't have to pay it back. You pay the money back if and when and in what amounts you want to. Forget the FICO scores and bank loan applications. The "what are you using the money for". Forget about it. You have access to your money at any time for any reason.

And this gets even better. Your money, your savings in your cash value life insurance policy is always growing. Everyday. Every minute no matter what. One of the big misunderstandings is you are not borrowing your money. You are borrowing the money from the insurance company of the insurance company's money. The insurance company is loaning you their money at a very low rate, less then banks would charge, and if the money is used for a business purpose it may be tax deductible, because they can get paid back out of your money in the policy, your cash value need be, but your money is always growing. Compare this to when you pull your money out of your savings account – it's over your money is earning no interest – it's gone you spent it. In a cash value life insurance policy your money always stays there and is always growing. How great is that?

If a smart deal comes along, you have the money. People say, I can make more money with it, which perhaps at times you can, so if you think you can, get a loan and use it. In reality, this ends up making you a better business person because you start weighting the risks and the returns you get from just leaving it in the policy without incurring the low loan interest rate the insurance company is charging.

With most investments, you can not readily access their value. Money invested in stocks if sold requires thinking about which stocks should be sold and what the tax hit will be if you do. Money in real estate takes time to sell or borrow against, and again requires thought about the tax consequences. What it really comes down to is your investment is a "paper asset", not really an asset you can use. Almost like it ceases to exist. Money in a cash value life insurance policy is different and unique, in that you can access the investment, your cash, when you want it or need it with a telephone call. You are your own banker. You also have the flexibility to stop and start making payments to the plan as will be discussed later.

This ability to control access to your money without government restriction and without taxation has so many practical real life benefits. One benefit might be you can afford to delay getting social security until age 70 and thus get the maximum payments from it by borrowing from your cash value.

Another benefit is your cash value can be used or not used to pay for college tuition. In the government's 529 plan the money in that plan to avoid income tax has to be used within a short period of time for college tuition and is counted against your child's application for student loans. The same money placed in a cash value life insurance policy may be used to pay college tuition or not, it's up to you, and the money is not counted against you when applying for student loans.

D. <u>Longevity</u>

Our plan is a lifetime plan. Some policies are called "whole life" to reflect that point. You are in this plan for life and want to be. You are free from the worries which most families live with. You know how much money you will have when you retire, you are your own banker having access to your savings when you need or want it in the meanwhile. No more loan applications, what is your FICO score, why do you want the money, when are you going to pay it back. No more tax hits on the money you have already paid taxes on. Tax-free, financial freedom is the plan and is the one you want to always be in.

A real benefit of the plan's longevity is you know how much money you have and you know how much death benefit you will leave for your family. Knowing there is a death benefit, you don't feel so bad about spending your money on yourself. This frees you up to getting reverse mortgages, spending your savings on vacations, on the "golden years" life style of your dreams, that red Corvette, whatever, because you know you are leaving your family a big check in the end called the beneficiary death benefit and it will be tax free to them and paid right away.

Without being in the plan most likely there will be no death benefit payout or the freedoms described of knowing you have it, because most term insurance policies are not renewable at old ages when you are most likely to die, and what term policies that may be available will be at such a high premium cost it makes no sense.

With our plan we can plan it out and make adjustments along the way depending on what did or did not happen in your life time. A good example is the flexibility to create what amounts to a tax free annuity that you can use or not use as you go along. Unlike annuity policies which lock you in to a fixed payout that requires income taxes paid on the payouts, with our plan we can get more or less, pay no taxes, start or stop it, or let the money and death benefit just grow and grow without any further payment which is what you might do if it turns out the money saved outside of the plan is enough.

You can then either just let your savings and death benefit grow and live off your other assets, exhausting them fully if you want to, knowing what you have in the plan, or you could start drawing off your cash value periodically or regularly like an annuity, but unlike and annuity you are not paying income tax on the money you pay yourself and you are not restricted as to how much you can get. Right there you can see our plan is better than any annuity. 30% or better just in tax savings alone.

Take a look at <u>Illustration #6</u>. Payments are made into the plan starting at age 40 for 28 years and then stopped at age 68. You can then either just let your savings grow or start your "annuity". In the policies I recommend, commonly called Indexed Universal Life, you can stop paying premiums or pay different amounts and the cash value alone keeps the policy going which is a good feature if you were to lose your job or otherwise unable to keep saving money. In Illustration #6, yearly withdrawals started at age 75, which in my experience is when many people need the money the most because they are running out of their savings and medical bills for doctors, medicine, home care medicare does not begin to cover, starts to spiral up with no end in sight. In Illustration #6, $150,000.00 was taken out every year for 20 years from age 75 until age 95. $3,000,000.00. How nice is that?

Besides having access to your money when needed or to take advantage of generating greater profits like when the real estate market tanks, paying no income taxes, and all the other benefits we discussed including being your own banker and not worrying about your future and running out of money, you see in Illustration #6, $624,400.00 was put in, $3,000,000.00 was taken out by 20 yearly payments of $150,000.00 and $1,096,888.00 is left as a tax free death benefit, and you stopped making contributions when you retired at 68. How's that? You put $624,400.00 in and getting back $4,096,888.00.

Illustrations#6 $624,400 in and get back $4,096,888.00

Age	Year	Premium	Premium totals	Loans	Policy value	Death Benefit
41	1	$22,300	$ 22,300	0	$15,904	2,000000
42	2	$22,300	$ 44,600	0	$32,304	2,000000
43	3	$22,300	$ 66,900	0	$49,731	2,000000
44	4	$22,300	$ 89,200	0	$68,287	2,000000
45	5	$22,300	$111,500	0	$88,042	2,000000
46	6	$22,300	$133,800	0	$109,027	2,000000
47	7	$22,300	$156,100	0	$131,340	2,000000
48	8	$22,300	$178,400	0	$155,098	2,000000
49	9	$22,300	$200,700	0	$180,445	2,000000
50	10	$22,300	$223,000	0	$207,452	2,000000
51	11	$22,300	$245,000	0	$243,637	2,000000
52	12	$22,300	$267,000	0	$282,200	2,000000
53	13	$22,300	$289,900	0	$323,283	2,000000
54	14	$22,300	$312,200	0	$367,055	2,000000
55	15	$22,300	$334,500	0	$413,682	2,000000

56	16	$22,300	$356,800	0	$463,370	2,000000
57	17	$22,300	$379,100	0	$516,336	2,000000
58	18	$22,300	$401,400	0	$572,813	2,000000
59	19	$22,300	$423,700	0	$633,000	2,000000
60	20	$22,300	$446,000	0	$697,338	2,000000
61	21	$22,300	$468,300	0	$765,882	2,000000
62	22	$22,300	$490,600	0	$838,982	2,000000
63	23	$22,300	$512,900	0	$916,948	2,000000
64	24	$22,300	$535,200	0	1,000147	2,000000
65	25	$22,300	$557,500	0	1,089085	2,000000
66	26	$22,300	$579,800	0	1,183974	2,000000
67	27	$22,300	$602,100	0	1,285637	2,000000
68	28	$22,300	$624,400	0	1,394667	2,000000
69	29	0	$624,400	0	1,488199	2,000000
70	30	0	$624,400	0	1,588621	2,000000
71	31	0	$624,400	0	1,696533	2,000000
72	32	0	$624,400	0	1,812539	2,000000
73	33	0	$624,400	0	1,937344	2,111705
74	34	0	$624,400	0	2,070913	2,215877
75	35	0	$624,400	$150,000	2,053642	2,156323
76	36	0	$624,400	$150,000	2,035491	2,137266
77	37	0	$624,000	$150,000	2,015901	2,116696
78	38	0	$624,400	$150,000	1,994735	2,094472
79	39	0	$624,400	$150,000	1,971501	2,076481

80	40	0	$624,400	$150,000	1,946126	2,057616
81	41	0	$624,400	$150,000	1,918350	2,036385
82	42	0	$624,400	$150,000	1,889888	2,012490
83	43	0	$624,400	$150,000	1,854424	1,985608
84	44	0	$624,400	$150,000	1,817599	1,955362
85	45	0	$624,400	$150,000	1,777009	1,921331
86	46	0	$624,400	$150,000	1,732235	1,883077
87	47	0	$624,400	$150,000	1,682719	1,840019
88	48	0	$624,400	$150,000	1,627875	1,791547
89	49	0	$624,400	$150,000	1,567071	1,736998
90	50	0	$624,400	$150,000	1,499618	1,675653
91	51	0	$624,400	$150,000	1,424854	1,570429
92	52	0	$624,400	$150,000	1,346423	1,459171
93	53	0	$624,400	$150,000	1,264986	1,342546
94	54	0	$624,400	$150,000	1,181418	1,221415
95	55	0	$624,400	$150,000	1,096888	1,096888
96	56	0	$624,400	0	1,173567	1,173567
97	57	0	$624,400	0	1,255617	1,255617
98	58	0	$624,400	0	1,343411	1,343411
99	59	0	$624,400	0	1,437872	1,437352

With 20 yearly payments to you as shown in Illustration #6, the first few policy years the growth is slow to cover the upfront costs of the plan, but it had little effect on the long term payout and is a small price to pay to be in the plan. All costs and fees are included in the projections, which are based on a 7.75% annual interest rate, which is less than the historical 9.03% return shown on Illustration #5. Your likely return will be greater than shown.

How's that compared to the uncertainty and lifetime worry about your retirement and how you are going to do it, all the while living with FICO scores and loan applications and never having financial piece of mind?

Another way to do this is to make lump sum payments in the beginning, while you have the money, and never make any more payments. Uncle Sam does not like that and slows you down by requiring the payments be made over the first five year period. Illustration #7 shows what is called a "seven pay over a five year period" of $336,169.22, which was the amount you would have liked to pay on day #1. $336,169.22 was put in, no other payments where ever made, and $3,000,000.00 was taken out by 20 yearly payments of $150,000.00 paid to you, and $1,478,702.00 is left as a tax free death benefit. Doing it this way, you put in $336,169.22 and paid back $4,478,702.00.

Illustrations#7 $336,169.22 in and get back $4,478,702.00

Age	Year	Premium	Premium totals	Loans	Policy value	Death Benefit
41	1	$79,146	$79,146	0	$74,274	2,000000
42	2	$79,146	$158,292	0	$151,937	2,000000
43	3	$79,146	$237,438	0	$234,944	2,000000
44	4	$79,146	$316,584	0	$323,707	2,000000
45	5	$19,585	$336,169	0	$358,730	2,000000
46	6	0	$336,169	0	$376,385	2,000000
47	7	0	$336,169	0	$385,154	2,000000
48	8	0	$336,169	0	$415,136	2,000000
49	9	0	$336,169	0	$436,450	2,000000
50	10	0	$336,169	0	$459,158	2,000000
51	11	0	$336,169	0	$489,803	2,000000
52	12	0	$336,169	0	$522,457	2,000000
53	13	0	$336,169	0	$557,240	2,000000
54	14	0	$336,169	0	$594,294	2,000000
55	15	0	$336,169	0	$633,758	2,000000
56	16	0	$336,169	0	$675,805	2,000000

57	17	0	$336,169	0	$720,618	2,000000
58	18	0	$336,169	0	$768,394	2,000000
59	19	0	$336,169	0	$819,349	2,000000
60	20	0	$336,169	0	$873,704	2,000000
61	21	0	$336,169	0	$931,653	2,000000
62	22	0	$336,169	0	$993,438	2,000000
63	23	0	$336,169	0	1,059318	2,000000
64	24	0	$336,169	0	1,129599	2,000000
65	25	0	$336,169	0	1,204708	2,000000
66	26	0	$336,169	0	1,284810	2,000000
67	27	0	$336,169	0	1,370610	2,000000
68	28	0	$336,169	0	1,462606	2,000000
69	29	0	$336,169	0	1,561345	2,000000
70	30	0	$336,169	0	1,667412	2,000000
71	31	0	$336,169	0	1,781457	2,013046
72	32	0	$336,169	0	1,904039	2,113484
73	33	0	$336,169	0	2,035151	2,218314
74	34	0	$336,169	0	2,175469	2,327752
75	35	0	$336,169	$150,000	2,165425	2,262778
76	36	0	$336,169	$150,000	2,155027	2,262778
77	37	0	$336,169	$150,000	2,143422	2,256398
78	38	0	$336,169	$150,000	2,130586	2,250687
79	39	0	$336,169	$150,000	2,116378	2,243691
80	40	0	$336,169	$150,000	2,100584	2,235186

81	41	0	$336,169	$150,000	2,082945	2,224907
82	42	0	$336,169	$150,000	2,063192	2,212572
83	43	0	$336,169	$150,000	2,041034	2,197880
84	44	0	$336,169	$150,000	2,016120	2,180467
85	45	0	$336,169	$150,000	1,988064	2,159928
86	46	0	$336,169	$150,000	1,956459	2,135842
87	47	0	$336,169	$150,000	1,920744	2,107623
88	48	0	$336,169	$150,000	1,880331	2,074656
89	49	0	$336,169	$150,000	1,834579	2,036274
90	50	0	$336,169	$150,000	1,782793	1,991747
91	51	0	$336,169	$150,000	1,724309	1,897170
92	52	0	$336,169	$150,000	1,663585	1,797558
93	53	0	$336,169	$150,000	1,601548	1,693803
94	54	0	$336,169	$150,000	1,539399	1,587037
95	55	0	$336,169	$150,000	1,478702	1,478702
96	56	0	$336,169	0	1,582116	1,582116
97	57	0	$336,169	0	1,692772	1,692772
98	58	0	$336,169	0	1,811176	1,811176
99	59	0	$336,169	0	1,937870	1,937870

Ideally, the 7 pay over the first 5 years is the best way to go, and is how wealthy people who have the money do it. More of your money gets into the plan quicker, giving you quicker access to more of your money and is more profitable. Instead of putting in $624,400.00 you put in only $336,169.22 and the payback was better - $4,478,702.00 instead of $4,096,888.00. As a practical matter, if you can make the commitment at the beginning, you pay less and get more out of your plan and it's over with. You are all set. Enjoy a life of financial freedom.

VIII. STARTING THE PLAN

Going back to the beginning, at what age do you want to retire and with how much money? With this information, your financial planner, <u>maybe</u> will suggest the best cash value life insurance policy on the market to accomplish this plan, if she/he is not limited to just selling the policies of the insurance company they work for, and will show you illustrations of how big the death benefit has to be and how much the contributions have to be to get you there.

Assuming it's the best policy available as I would recommend, a possible hurdle could be the insurance company does not want to insure you for as much as you want to enable your payments to produce the retirement income you want, when you want it. What can you do? What wealthy people do, including those in bad health who cannot get life insurance, is they insure their spouse, their children, their relatives, all the while being the owner and beneficiary of these policies with complete control over them, until the amount of premium is projected to generate the amount of income they want at the age they want it.

You see the idea is not to pay as little as possible for the life insurance which is the typical life insurance agent's sales pitch, the idea is to put in as much as you can to meet your plan's goal.

The more you can put into savings in the policy the sooner you will be retired with money. Let that serve as an incentive.

The biggest mistake you can make now is not starting now.

IX. CONCLUSION

Cash value life insurance, particularly today's best cash value life insurance policies geared to living benefits for you, allows you to accumulate a substantial amount of cash that you have access to at any time, for any reason, without penalties, is unrelated to the stock market up's and down's, and will generate a retirement income that is not included in your tax returns.

Today's cash value life insurance policies are not only the safest, most predictable, proven, best way to go, but are also the least known and most misunderstood savings tool offered to the general public. Thank goodness Walt Disney knew about it and thank goodness you now know.

You now know the way to go and with this knowledge you are ready to make your plan. If you contact me, I can help you make your plan.

Remember you are never too old to set a new goal or to make a new dream and with the magic of compounding interest, tax free earnings and the guarantee you will not lose money, the sooner you start, the sooner you will be where you want to be.

Wishing you the retirement of your dreams.

Jorn S. Rossi Esq.

Rossilaw@yahoo.com

About the author

Jorn S. Rossi, is a California licensed attorney at law since 1979. Mr. Rossi's area of practice is estate planning and he is a current member of the Trusts & Estates section of the California State bar. For over 30 years Mr. Rossi has advised individuals and families on estate planning methods to advance their financial and personal goals. Mr. Rossi is also a Series 6 financial planner, an accident, health & life insurance agent, a real estate broker, and notary public. Mr. Rossi is a featured seminar speaker on estate planning and retirement plans. Mr. Rossi earned a Bachelor of Business Administration B.B.A. Degree from Pace University, and a Juris Doctor J.D. degree from Western State University, College of Law.

www.ingramcontent.com/pod-product-compliance
Lightning Source LLC
Chambersburg PA
CBHW030053230526
45471CB00003B/1084